For further information about
Action Books, please write to:

Barrie & Jenkins Ltd.,
24 Highbury Crescent,
London N5 1RX

Chancerel Publishers Ltd.,
40 Tavistock Street,
London WC2E 7PB

ISBN 0-905703-23-5

Photoset by Tottenham Typesetters, London
Printed in Italy

action

BOOKS

GOLF
100 ways to improve your game

TENNIS
Basic techniques and tactics

PHOTOGRAPHY
Using a 35 mm camera

YOGA
The happy way to live

JUDO
The practical way

MOTORCYCLES
Maintain your own machine

SWIMMING
Learning, training, competing

MOTORCARS
Maintenance and minor repairs

HOME MOVIES
Make and project your own films

COOKERY
Skills of French cuisine

FREEZING
Save time, money and eat well

BASKETBALL
Scoring skills and strategies

CHESS
Master the moves

WOODWORKING
Tools, techniques and projects

KNITTING
Patterns, stitches and styles

FOOTBALL
Match winning skills and tactics

OWNING A DOG
Choosing, rearing and training

HOUSE PLANTS
Care and cultivation

COARSE FISHING
Bait, tackle and technique

COARSE FISHING
Bait, tackle and technique

Text by Fred Rashbrook
Drawings by Claude-Henri Juillard

Chancerel | **BARRIE & JENKINS**
COMMUNICA-EUROPA

Contents

REELS 9
Adjusting the reel brake 10
Tightening the reel handle 10
Inspection and maintenance of reels 11
Running repairs 11
Loading the spool correctly 12
A backing problem 12
Spilling line 14
Braking in time 14
Using the anti-reverse lever 15
Untwisting a line 15
Winding on a new line 16

RODS 19
Fishing in the rain 20
Beware of worn tip rings 20
Measuring fish 21
Personalised rods 21
Dry rods carefully 22
Loose whipping 22
Whipping on a rod ring 24
Gluing the whipping 24
Loose reel mounting 25
Uncoupling rod sections 25
Easing tight ferrules 26
Worn ferrules 26
Wear on glass fibre ferrules 28
Carrying a rod correctly 28

BAITS AND LURES 31
Mixing groundbait 32
The clinker trick 32
Cleaning maggots 33
Cheese-flavoured maggots 33
Keeping maggots healthy 34
Transporting livebait 34
Preserving deadbait 36
Sweetcorn for carp 36
Long distance groundbaiting 37
Meat for lunch 37
Cooking wheat the easy way 38
Bait with hempseed 38
Hemp and tares 40
Preparing groundbait 40
Swimfeeders 41
Floating crusts 41
Making breadpaste 42
Collecting lobworms 42
Storing lobworms 44
Bait for barbel, bream and carp 44
Bait for chub, dace and perch 45
Bait for pike, roach and tench 45

HOOKS, LINES AND LEADERS 47
Shotting the float 48
Tying an eyed hook 48
Joining leader to fly line 49
Sorting out spools and winders 49
Marking spools and winders 50
Straightening out a fly cast 50
Extracting a hook 52
A tip guard for hooks 52
Storing nylon line 53
Marking a fly reel 53
Loops on wire traces—making
  the loop 54
Threading a sleeve on to a wire
  trace 54
Sharpening hooks 56
Keeping tied hooks tidy 56

TERMINAL TACKLE   59
Shock absorber for leger weight   60
Stop knot for sliding float   60
Bite indicators   61
Bite indicators for windy weather   61
Paternoster leger rig   62
Fast river legering   62
Preparing weights   64
Livebaiting   64
Tying a dropper knot   65
Tackle and fly boxes   65

REPAIRS AND ODD JOBS   67
Restoring a worn fly   68
Tidy swivels   68
Making a float—cutting out   69
Making a float—finishing off   69
A cheap bailer   70
Interchangeable float caps   70
A minnow trap   72
Keep hooks rust free   72
Forceps at the ready   74
When maggots turn   74
Leaky waders   76
Leaky boots   76
Repairing rubber boots   78
A do-it-yourself plummet   78
A handy bait box   80
Don't lose your sunglasses   80
Mounting a pike head-preparation   81
Mounting a pike head–the mount   81

READING THE WATER   83
Spotting likely hotspots   84
Where to find perch   84
Where to find carp and tench   86
Where to find dace   86
Where to find chub   88
Where to find roach   88

GLOSSARY   90
METRICATION   91
PHOTOGRAPHS   92
BIOGRAPHY   93

Reels

Correct handling and adjustment of the reel
can mean the difference between landing or
losing your fish. In fact, the reel is a vital
piece of equipment that must be carefully
loaded and maintained to ensure that it
works smoothly just when you want it to.

Adjusting the reel brake

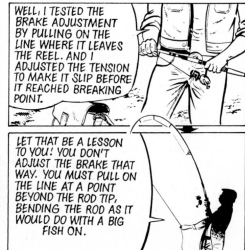

Tightening the reel handle

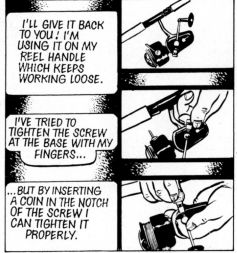

Inspection and maintenance of reels

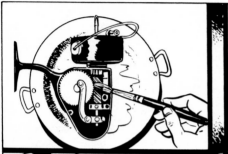  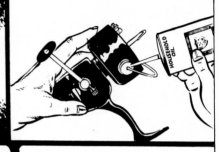

IF YOU WANT TO KEEP YOUR REEL IN GOOD WORKING ORDER, FOR LONG AND TROUBLE-FREE SERVICE, OVERHAUL IT AT LEAST ONCE A YEAR, AT THE END OF THE SEASON. FIRST UNSCREW THE CASE. USE A SOFT BRUSH AND PETROL TO CLEAN OUT THE INSIDE AND GET RID OF THE OLD OIL.

THEN PUT IN NEW OIL— JUST ENOUGH TO COAT THE GEARS. TOO MUCH OIL SERVES NO USEFUL PURPOSE.

AFTER REPLACING THE COVER, ADD A COUPLE OF DROPS OF OIL TO EACH END OF THE BALE ARM, THE ANTI-REVERSE LEVER, THE WINDING HANDLE, ETC.

Running repairs

GEORGE, I FELL DOWN AND BENT THE BALE ARM ON MY REEL. NOW IT'S RUBBING AGAINST THE SPOOL.

THAT'S NOT TOO SERIOUS REALLY. I'LL FIX IT FOR YOU. SEE, I'M CAREFULLY PRESSING THE BALE ARM BACK INTO SHAPE. YOU CAN CARRY ON FISHING NOW.

Loading the spool correctly

HOW DO YOU CAST SO FAR SO EASILY, GEORGE?

INCORRECT

SHOW ME YOUR REEL. JUST AS I THOUGHT—YOUR SPOOL IS BADLY LOADED. AS A RESULT YOUR LINE IS RUBBING AGAINST THE EDGES EACH TIME YOU CAST. IT SHOULD BE LOADED TO WITHIN ABOUT ONE EIGHTH OF AN INCH FROM THE LIP OF THE SPOOL.

CORRECT

TALKING ABOUT THAT, YOU ASKED ME WHAT A REEL "SKIRT" IS. WELL, THAT'S WHAT IT IS— A CHENILLE EXTENSION OF THE SPOOL DESIGNED TO PREVENT THE LINE FROM GETTING SNAGGED UNDER-NEATH THE EDGE. UNFORTUNATELY, NOT ALL REELS ARE MADE THAT WAY.

A backing problem

CHANGING YOUR LINE AGAIN? YOU ONLY CHANGED IT TEN DAYS AGO.

EACH TIME I CAST, THE FIRST TEN METRES ARE OKAY, THEN THE LINE STARTS GETTING TWISTED AND TANGLED UP ON ITSELF ROUND THE SPOOL.

I SEE. YOU HAVEN'T WOUND A PIECE OF ADHESIVE TAPE ROUND YOUR BACKING LINE, LIKE THAT.

NOW YOU CAN RELOAD THE SPOOL WITHOUT YOUR FISHING LINE CATCHING ON THE BACKING!

Spilling line

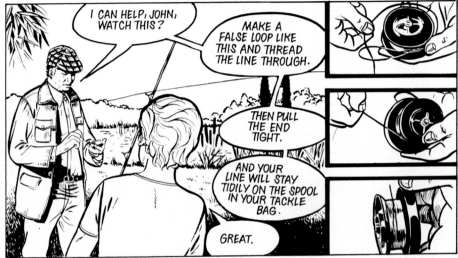

Braking in time

Using the anti-reverse lever

THIS REEL IS GETTING ME DOWN WITH THE NOISE IT MAKES. I OILED IT THOROUGHLY BUT THE RATCHET IS TOO NOISY. YOUR REEL DOESN'T MAKE THAT NOISE, GEORGE.

WHIRR WHIRR

THERE'S NOTHING WRONG WITH YOUR REEL.

10

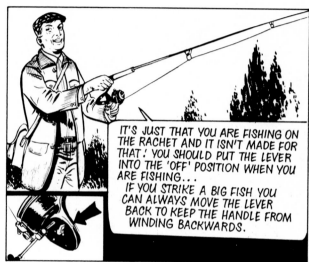

IT'S JUST THAT YOU ARE FISHING ON THE RACHET AND IT ISN'T MADE FOR THAT! YOU SHOULD PUT THE LEVER INTO THE 'OFF' POSITION WHEN YOU ARE FISHING...
IF YOU STRIKE A BIG FISH YOU CAN ALWAYS MOVE THE LEVER BACK TO KEEP THE HANDLE FROM WINDING BACKWARDS.

Untwisting a line

WHY ARE YOU LAYING OUT YOUR LINE ON THE GRASS, GEORGE?

BECAUSE IT HAS BECOME TWISTED AND IS FORMING INTO LOOPS WHEN I CAST.

NOW THAT I'VE GOT IT COMPLETELY STRETCHED OUT, ALL I HAVE TO DO IS WIND IT BACK ON TO THE SPOOL. AS IT IS DRAWN ALONG THE GRASS IT UNRAVELS ITSELF. IF YOU HAPPEN TO BE IN A BOAT, YOU CAN TRAIL THE LINE BEHIND IT IN THE WATER AND THIS WILL TAKE OUT THE TWISTS IN THE SAME WAY.

11

Winding on a new line

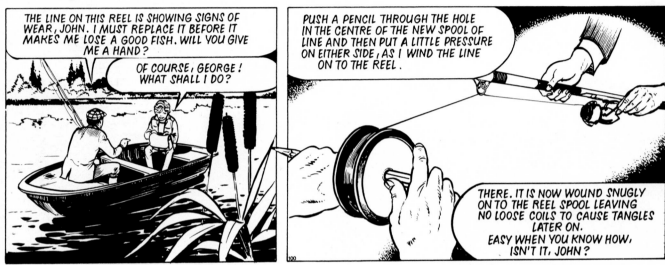

Rods

The use of fibre glass instead of cane for
fishing rods has solved many angling
problems. A modern fibre glass rod is tough,
light and weatherproof, and can stand great
pressures. Your rod can last a lifetime, if
you know how to look after it, with carefui
storing and cleaning, checking ferrules for
wear and, when necessary, renewing rod
rings and reel mountings.

Fishing in the rain

Beware of worn tip rings

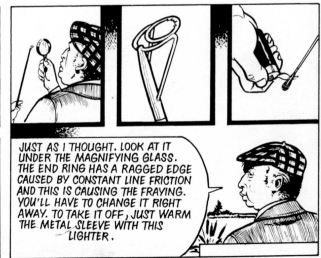

Measuring fish

GEORGE, COME QUICKLY! I'VE GOT A FISH BUT I THINK IT IS UNDER-SIZED AND I'VE FORGOTTEN MY TAPE MEASURE.

HANG ON A MINUTE!

YOU SEE, I DON'T NEED A TAPE MEASURE.

I'VE ALREADY MADE MARKS ON MY ROD TO SHOW THE FISH SIZE LIMITS. A COAT OF VARNISH ON TOP PREVENTS THE MARKS FROM WEARING OFF.

SIZE LIMITS FOR FRESHWATER FISH VARY FROM AREA TO AREA.
SO CHECK THE LOCAL RULES.

Personalised rods

I WAS ADMIRING YOUR NEW ROD JUST NOW, GEORGE AND I NOTICED THAT YOU HAD YOUR NAME ON IT.

YOU CAN DO THE SAME ON YOURS.

103

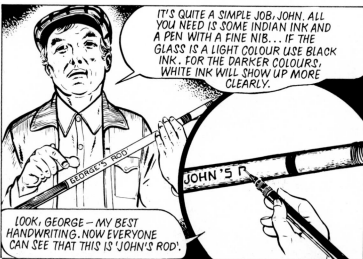

IT'S QUITE A SIMPLE JOB, JOHN. ALL YOU NEED IS SOME INDIAN INK AND A PEN WITH A FINE NIB... IF THE GLASS IS A LIGHT COLOUR USE BLACK INK. FOR THE DARKER COLOURS, WHITE INK WILL SHOW UP MORE CLEARLY.

GEORGE'S ROD

JOHN'S R

LOOK, GEORGE — MY BEST HANDWRITING. NOW EVERYONE CAN SEE THAT THIS IS 'JOHN'S ROD'.

Dry rods carefully

WE'VE GOT A BIT OF DRYING OUT TO DO WHEN WE GET HOME—EVERYTHING IS SOAKED. AT LEAST OUR RODS CAN'T COME TO MUCH HARM, CAN THEY, GEORGE?

104

THEY NEED PROPER CARE LIKE THE REST OF YOUR EQUIPMENT, JOHN. THEY SHOULD NEVER BE LEFT IN A WET ROD BAG. GIVE THE ROD SECTIONS A GOOD WIPE OVER WITH A SOFT DRY CLOTH.

AND THEN PUT THEM BACK IN THE BAG WHEN IT HAS THOROUGHLY DRIED OUT. THIS HELPS TO MAKE SURE THAT THE ROD FITTINGS DON'T TARNISH OR RUST

Loose whipping

YOU'RE GOING TO LOSE THAT ROD RING—THE WHIPPING IS SO WORN AND FRAYED.

16

FOR THE TIME BEING WE'LL WRAP SOME TAPE AROUND IT. WE'LL DO IT AGAIN AT HOME THIS EVENING WITH PROPER BINDING TAPE.

HERE'S YOUR ROD BACK YOU CAN FISH WITHOUT WORRY NOW.

THANKS, GEORGE!

Whipping on a rod ring

NOW WE'RE HOME, JOHN, I'LL SHOW YOU HOW TO WHIP ON YOUR OWN ROD RINGS WHEN NECESSARY.

YES, GEORGE, I'VE NEVER REALLY GOT THE HANG OF IT.

FIRST, POSITION THE RING ACCURATELY ON THE ROD AND FASTEN IT THERE WITH WITH A PIECE OF ADHESIVE TAPE OVER ONE 'LEG'.
START THE WHIPPING UP THE OTHER 'LEG' BY TURNING THE ROD WITH THE LEFT HAND.

JUST BEFORE COMPLETING ALL THE TURNS, PUT A SEPARATE LOOP OF THREAD UNDER THE LAST FEW TURNS SO THAT YOU CAN PULL THROUGH THE END OF THE WHIPPING THREAD, TIGHTEN IT UP AND TRIM IT OFF NEATLY.

116

NOW I'LL HAVE TO PRACTISE MYSELF.

Gluing the whipping

I SEE YOU'RE FINISHING OFF WHIPPING ON ANOTHER ROD RING.

21

YES I'M JUST GLUING IT... I'LL WAIT FOR THE GLUE TO SET AND THEN...

...AND SMOOTH IT OUT.

I'LL SPREAD IT WELL OVER THE WHIPPING WITH THE FLAT SIDE OF MY KNIFE...

FINISHED! LET IT DRY AND THEN THE ROD RING SHOULD STAY FIRMLY IN PLACE.

Loose reel mounting

WHAT'S HAPPENING TO YOUR REEL, JOHN? IT'S SLIPPING ABOUT. IF YOU LOSE THIS PIKE YOU'LL HAVE ONLY YOURSELF TO BLAME

QUICK! IT'S GOING TO GET AWAY AND IT'S NOT MY FAULT— THE REEL FITTING KEEPS LOOSENING UP ON ME.

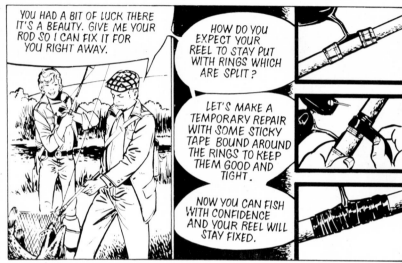

YOU HAD A BIT OF LUCK THERE IT'S A BEAUTY. GIVE ME YOUR ROD SO I CAN FIX IT FOR YOU RIGHT AWAY.

HOW DO YOU EXPECT YOUR REEL TO STAY PUT WITH RINGS WHICH ARE SPLIT?

LET'S MAKE A TEMPORARY REPAIR WITH SOME STICKY TAPE BOUND AROUND THE RINGS TO KEEP THEM GOOD AND TIGHT.

NOW YOU CAN FISH WITH CONFIDENCE AND YOUR REEL WILL STAY FIXED.

Uncoupling rod sections

I CAN'T SEPARATE THESE TWO SECTIONS. CAN YOU HELP?

GRASP THE SECTION IN FRONT WITH YOUR LEFT HAND AND THE ONE BEHIND WITH YOUR RIGHT. LEAVE ME A SPACE TO DO THE SAME. ON THE COUNT OF THREE, WE'LL BOTH PULL APART AT THE SAME TIME. 1...2...3... AND THERE YOU ARE.

WHEN YOU ARE ON YOUR OWN, YOU CAN OFTEN MANAGE TO SEPARATE THEM BY GETTING EXTRA PRESSURE ON YOUR HANDS FROM YOUR THIGHS—LIKE THIS.

GEORGE'S DONE IT AGAIN.

Easing tight ferrules

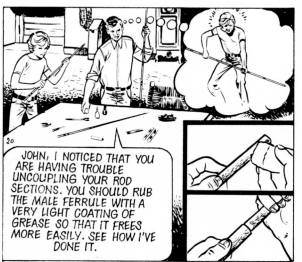

JOHN, I NOTICED THAT YOU ARE HAVING TROUBLE UNCOUPLING YOUR ROD SECTIONS. YOU SHOULD RUB THE MALE FERRULE WITH A VERY LIGHT COATING OF GREASE SO THAT IT FREES MORE EASILY. SEE HOW I'VE DONE IT.

AT THE NEXT FISHING SESSION

LOOK, GEORGE, TODAY MY ROD IS COMPLETELY STRAIGHT AND IT WAS EASY TO PUT TOGETHER TOO.

ALL THESE LITTLE DETAILS ARE IMPORTANT TO YOUR FISHING!

YES, AND HERE'S THE PROOF! LOOK AT MY KEEPNET. A GOOD CATCH DON'T YOU THINK?

Worn ferrules

MORE WORK FOR YOU, GEORGE! ALL MY ROD JOINTS NEED ATTENTION, JUST AS YOU SAID.

YOU MUST LEARN TO SET ASIDE TIME FOR MAINTENANCE ON YOUR EQUIPMENT IF YOU WANT TO AVOID PROBLEMS WHEN YOU ARE OUT FISHING!

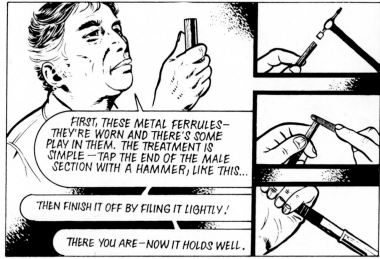

FIRST, THESE METAL FERRULES— THEY'RE WORN AND THERE'S SOME PLAY IN THEM. THE TREATMENT IS SIMPLE — TAP THE END OF THE MALE SECTION WITH A HAMMER, LIKE THIS...

THEN FINISH IT OFF BY FILING IT LIGHTLY!

THERE YOU ARE—NOW IT HOLDS WELL.

Wear on glass fibre ferrules

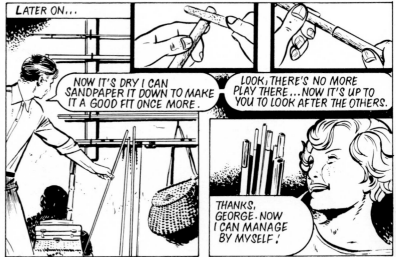

Carrying a rod correctly

Baits and lures

Before you can catch a fish, you have to tempt it to bite. So the quality and freshness of the bait—groundbait or hookbait—is important. You'll discover that, like you, fish have favourite tastes. So study the water, find the fish and decide which bait is best to make it bite.

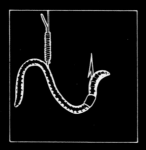

Mixing groundbait

IF YOU WANT YOUR GROUNDBAIT MIXTURE TO HAVE A SMOOTH AND EVEN CONSISTENCY SO THAT IT ATTRACTS THE FISH WITHOUT ACTUALLY FEEDING THEM, YOU MUST SIEVE IT AFTER WETTING IT.

NOW LOOK AT THE RESULT- THE INGREDIENTS ARE WELL MIXED AND THERE ARE NO LUMPS.

NOW YOU CAN MAKE BALLS OF GROUNDBAIT.

NOW I UNDERSTAND WHY THE FISH COME AND STAY IN YOUR SWIM!

The clinker trick

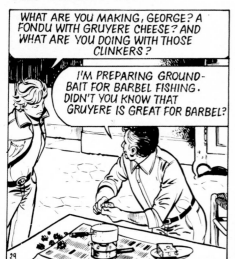

WHAT ARE YOU MAKING, GEORGE? A FONDU WITH GRUYERE CHEESE? AND WHAT ARE YOU DOING WITH THOSE CLINKERS?

I'M PREPARING GROUND- BAIT FOR BARBEL FISHING. DIDN'T YOU KNOW THAT GRUYERE IS GREAT FOR BARBEL?

THE TROUBLE IS THAT IF YOU TRY TO GROUNDBAIT WITH PIECES OF CHEESE THE CURRENT CARRIES THEM AWAY FROM THE SWIM. SO WHAT I DO IS TO MELT THE CHEESE AND ADD MY CLINKERS TO THE MIXTURE. THE HOLES FILL UP WITH MELTED CHEESE AND THEN BY TOMORROW MORNING THE CHEESE WILL HAVE COOLED DOWN...

I CAN THROW THE CLINKERS INTO THE CURRENT AND THEY WILL SINK TO THE BOTTOM AND THE BARBEL WILL BE ATTRACTED BY THE CHEESE, BUT THEY WON'T BE ABLE TO GET IT OUT OF THE HOLES. ALL I HAVE TO DO IS FISH AMONG THEM WITH MY HOOK BAITED WITH A CUBE OF CHEESE.

Cleaning maggots

YOU CAN HELP THESE MAGGOTS TO STAY ALIVE – WITHOUT SMELLING – IF YOU LOOK AFTER THEM A LITTLE. FIRST SIEVE THEM TO GET RID OF ANY RUBBISH...THEN...

WASH THEM IN LUKEWARM WATER, MOVING THEM AROUND AND RUBBING THEM GENTLY WITH YOUR FINGERS.

NOW THEY'RE CLEAN AND YOU MUST DRY THEM OFF, SO SPREAD THEM OUT ON A DRY CLOTH,...

ROLL UP THE CLOTH MAKING SURE THEY'RE WELL SPREAD OUT RATHER THAN PACKED TOGETHER!

TAKE UP THE SIDES OF THE CLOTH AND PRESS IT GENTLY ON THE MAGGOTS AND WHEN THEY'RE DRY, TAKE THEM OUT OF THE CLOTH AND PUT THEM INTO THE BAIT BOX.

Cheese-flavoured maggots

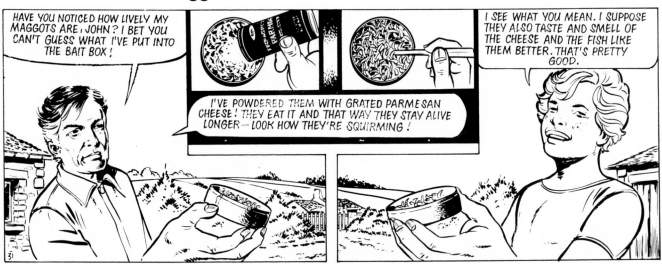

HAVE YOU NOTICED HOW LIVELY MY MAGGOTS ARE, JOHN? I BET YOU CAN'T GUESS WHAT I'VE PUT INTO THE BAIT BOX!

I'VE POWDERED THEM WITH GRATED PARMESAN CHEESE! THEY EAT IT AND THAT WAY THEY STAY ALIVE LONGER – LOOK HOW THEY'RE SQUIRMING!

I SEE WHAT YOU MEAN. I SUPPOSE THEY ALSO TASTE AND SMELL OF THE CHEESE AND THE FISH LIKE THEM BETTER. THAT'S PRETTY GOOD.

Keeping maggots healthy

Transporting livebait

Preserving deadbait

YOU MAY NOT BELIEVE IT, BUT DURING THE SUMMER I ALWAYS TRY TO CATCH A SUPPLY OF MINNOWS FOR BAIT FISHING. I LINE THEM UP ON ALUMINIUM FOIL AND COVER THEM WITH ANOTHER PIECE. THEN I FOLD OVER THE EDGES AND PUT THE PACKET INTO THE FREEZER. WHEN I WANT TO TAKE THEM OUT THEY'RE STILL PERFECT...

YOU CAN CATCH THEM LIKE THE KIDS DO, GEORGE!

YOU MAY LAUGH, BUT IT'S WORTH DOING—AND I DO THE SAME WITH OTHER SMALL FISH WHICH I USE AS DEADBAITS FOR PIKE AND ZANDER

Sweetcorn for carp

DON'T EAT ALL YOUR CORN ON THE COB, JOHN... SAVE SOME OF IT FOR WHEN WE GO TO THE CARP LAKE TOMORROW.

DON'T TELL ME CARP LIKE IT TOO?

YES, WE'LL THROW SOME OUT AS GROUND-BAIT FIRST... THEN JUST PUT A SINGLE PARTICLE OF CORN ON THE HOOK. HOW'S THAT?

I'VE GOT A BITE.

STRIKE QUICKLY... THAT'S A GOOD FISH I THINK.

I'M JOLLY GLAD I WASN'T TOO GREEDY AT SUPPER LAST NIGHT!

Long distance groundbaiting

GEORGE, I CAN'T THROW MY SWEET-CORN FAR ENOUGH TO ATTRACT THE CARP TO THE SPOT WHERE MY BAIT IS...

WATCH HOW I'M GETTING MINE OUT—WITH A CATAPULT. IT GOES A LONG WAY— AND ACCURATELY, TOO. TRY IT!

LOOK AT THAT! DID YOU SEE HOW FAR I SHOT IT? THAT'S GREAT. I'LL BRING A CATAPULT NEXT TIME, FOR SURE.

Meat for lunch

IF YOU'RE NOT GOING TO FINISH THAT LUNCHEON MEAT SANDWICH, I'LL HAVE IT. BUT I'M NOT GOING TO EAT IT MYSELF. I THINK THERE'S SOME BARBEL IN THIS SWIM AND THEY LOVE IT.

FISH EAT MEAT?

YES, INDEED. SEE, I CUT THE MEAT INTO SMALL CUBES AND I BURY THE HOOK IN ONE OF THEM LIKE THIS.

NOW WE JUST SIT BACK AND WAIT!

Cooking wheat the easy way

Baiting with hempseed

Hemp and tares

Preparing groundbait

Swimfeeders

WE NEED TO KEEP OUR GROUNDBAIT ON THE BOTTOM IN THIS FAST WATER SO THROWING IT OUT IN BALLS WON'T DO.

HOW SHALL WE MANAGE THEN?

108

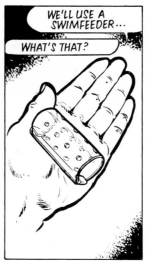

WE'LL USE A SWIMFEEDER...

WHAT'S THAT?

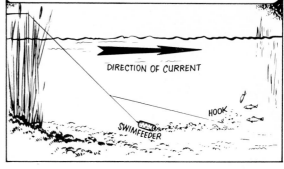

HERE YOU ARE...IT'S A PERFORATED CYLINDER OF CLEAR PLASTIC OPEN AT EACH END WHICH WE'LL ATTACH TO OUR LEGER RIG. WE STUFF IT FULL OF MAGGOTS AND GROUNDBAIT AND CAST IT OUT INTO THE SWIM ... THE GROUNDBAIT SLOWLY WASHES OUT AROUND THE HOOKBAIT AND THE FISH ARE ATTRACTED EXACTLY TO THE RIGHT SPOT!

DIRECTION OF CURRENT

HOOK

SWIMFEEDER

Floating crusts

I'M KEEPING SOME CRUSTS LEFT OVER FROM BAIT-MAKING—THEY'LL COME IN HANDY LATER DOWN ON THE LAKE.

WHAT ARE YOU GOING TO DO... FEED THE DUCKS?

NO, STUPID. THERE ARE SOME BIG, FAT CARP IN THAT WATER AND THEY ARE VERY PARTIAL TO BREADCRUST.

HOW DO YOU GET THEM TO TAKE IT?

JUST THROW A FEW LOOSE PIECES OUT AT FIRST TO TEMPT THEM, THEN GENTLY LOWER OUR CRUST-BAITED HOOK ONTO THE WATER AT THE EDGE OF THE REEDS... AND WAIT.

109

THERE! HE'S TAKING IT!

Making breadpaste

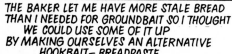

THE BAKER LET ME HAVE MORE STALE BREAD THAN I NEEDED FOR GROUNDBAIT SO I THOUGHT WE COULD USE SOME OF IT UP BY MAKING OURSELVES AN ALTERNATIVE HOOKBAIT — BREADPASTE.

IT ONLY TAKES A MINUTE OR TWO... JUST WRAP THE CRUMBS IN THIS PIECE OF CLEAN CLOTH... HOLD IT UNDER THE WATER TAP TO SOAK IT WELL... THEN SQUEEZE OUT THE SURPLUS WATER AND KNEAD THE BREAD INTO A SMOOTH PASTE... ROACH LOVE IT !

YOU SEE, JOHN, IT CERTAINLY PAYS TO USE YOUR LOAF IN ANGLING !

Collecting lobworms

WHY ARE YOU WATERING THE GRASS, GEORGE..? AND WHAT'S THAT POLE FOR?

THAT'S GOT YOU GUESSING, HASN'T IT? IT'S TO GIVE ME A SMALL SUPPLY OF LOBWORMS... TOMORROW MORNING YOU WILL SEE WHAT I MEAN...

DURING THE NIGHT — THANKS TO MY WATERING — THE WORMS HAVE COME TO THE SURFACE. NOW I FORCE THE POLE INTO THE EARTH AND SHAKE IT ABOUT VIGOROUSLY TO PRODUCE VIBRATIONS IN THE GROUND !

NEXT DAY.

THE WORMS COME OUT OF THE GROUND TO GET AWAY FROM THE VIBRATIONS AND ALL I HAVE TO DO NOW IS PICK THEM UP !

Storing lobworms

IF YOU WANT MOSS, GEORGE, I KNOW A TREE WHERE THERE'S PLENTY.

THIS IS FOR PRESERVING MY LOBWORMS AND THE MOSS WHICH GROWS ON TREES ISN'T AS GOOD AS THE STUFF YOU FIND IN DAMP PLACES ON THE GROUND.

WHAT'S MORE, I DON'T NEED A LOT, JUST ENOUGH TO FILL MY BOX. IF I MAKE SURE THAT THE MOSS STAYS DAMP, THE WORMS WILL KEEP WELL IN IT AND HARDEN. LOOK AT THIS ONE...

THAT'S WHY YOU ALWAYS HAVE SUCH GOOD LOBWORMS THEN. MINE ARE ALWAYS HALF DEAD AND LIMP ON THE HOOK. THAT ONE LOOKS REALLY LIVELY.

34

Bait for barbel, bream and carp

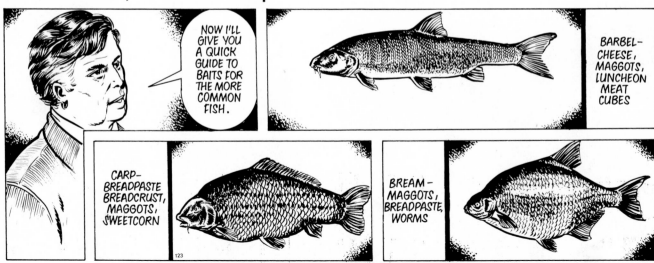

NOW I'LL GIVE YOU A QUICK GUIDE TO BAITS FOR THE MORE COMMON FISH.

BARBEL- CHEESE, MAGGOTS, LUNCHEON MEAT CUBES

CARP- BREADPASTE BREADCRUST, MAGGOTS, SWEETCORN

123

BREAM- MAGGOTS, BREADPASTE, WORMS

Bait for chub, dace and perch

CHUB –
MAGGOTS, BREADPASTE,
BREADFLAKE, CHEESE,
CHEESEPASTE, WORMS,
SLUGS

DACE –
MAGGOTS, CASTERS
(CHRYSALIDS),
FLIES

PERCH –
WORMS, MAGGOTS,
MINNOWS (LIVE OR
DEAD).

Bait for pike, roach and tench

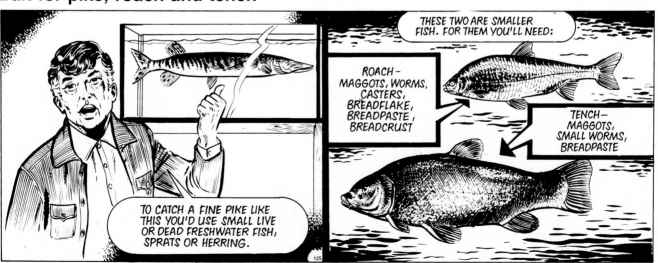

THESE TWO ARE SMALLER
FISH. FOR THEM YOU'LL NEED:

ROACH –
MAGGOTS, WORMS,
CASTERS,
BREADFLAKE,
BREADPASTE,
BREADCRUST

TENCH –
MAGGOTS,
SMALL WORMS,
BREADPASTE

TO CATCH A FINE PIKE LIKE
THIS YOU'D USE SMALL LIVE
OR DEAD FRESHWATER FISH,
SPRATS OR HERRING.

Hooks, lines and leaders

The baited hook is the end of the line for your catch, so it's important your hook should be sharp and strong. The line and trace should be well balanced and strong, but fine; capable of deceiving, catching and resisting the fighting power of, perhaps, a 20-pounder.

Shotting the float

Tying an eyed hook

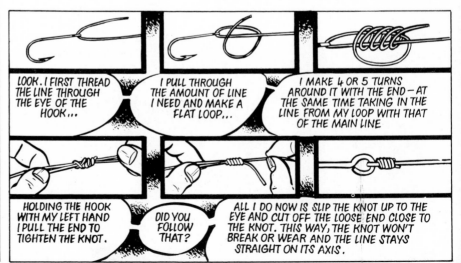

Joining leader to fly line

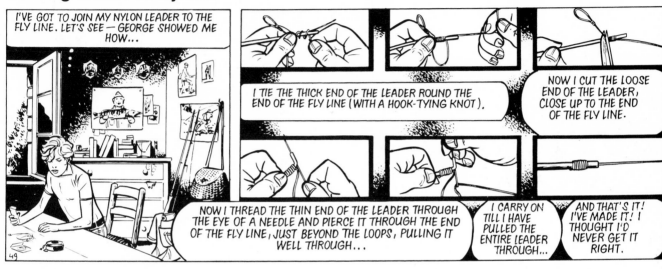

I'VE GOT TO JOIN MY NYLON LEADER TO THE FLY LINE. LET'S SEE — GEORGE SHOWED ME HOW...

I TIE THE THICK END OF THE LEADER ROUND THE END OF THE FLY LINE (WITH A HOOK-TYING KNOT).

NOW I CUT THE LOOSE END OF THE LEADER, CLOSE UP TO THE END OF THE FLY LINE.

NOW I THREAD THE THIN END OF THE LEADER THROUGH THE EYE OF A NEEDLE AND PIERCE IT THROUGH THE END OF THE FLY LINE, JUST BEYOND THE LOOPS, PULLING IT WELL THROUGH...

I CARRY ON TILL I HAVE PULLED THE ENTIRE LEADER THROUGH...

AND THAT'S IT! I'VE MADE IT! I THOUGHT I'D NEVER GET IT RIGHT.

Sorting out spools and winders

ALL THOSE LINES YOU'VE GOT! I OFTEN WONDER HOW YOU MANAGE TO KNOW WHICH IS WHICH, GEORGE.

IS IT 3lb OR 4 lb LINE I'VE GOT ON THIS SPOOL? I DON'T REMEMBER MYSELF NOW...

HOW DO I MANAGE? AND REMEMBER THE STRENGTH OF EACH LINE? QUITE SIMPLY I MARK EACH SPOOL AND EACH LINE WINDER.

Marking spools and winders

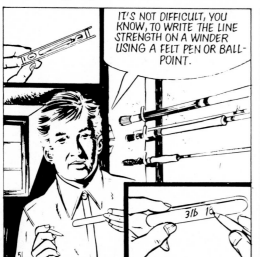

IT'S NOT DIFFICULT, YOU KNOW, TO WRITE THE LINE STRENGTH ON A WINDER USING A FELT PEN OR BALL-POINT.

WITH A SPOOL, IT ONLY TAKES A MINUTE OR TWO TO WRITE THE LINE STRENGTH ON A PIECE OF TAPE OR PAPER AND STICK IT ON. YOU YOUNG LADS ARE ALL THE SAME. YOU NEVER TAKE ENOUGH TIME TO DO THINGS PROPERLY, BUT ORGANISING YOUR TACKLE IS AN IMPORTANT PART OF FISHING, YOU KNOW.

YOU SOUND LIKE A SCHOOLTEACHER, GEORGE — BUT THANKS ANYWAY FOR THE ADVICE AND I'LL TRY TO BE A GOOD PUPIL!

Straightening out a fly cast

COME AND LOOK AT MY FLY CAST, GEORGE. IT'S BADLY TWISTED UP AND I HAVEN'T ANOTHER WITH ME.

MINE'S IN A SIMILAR STATE BUT I KNOW HOW TO PUT IT RIGHT. COME AND SEE HOW IT'S DONE.

I PULL THE UPPER PART OF THE CAST THROUGH THE FOLD OF THIS SMALL PIECE OF RUBBER WHICH I KEEP IN MY POCKET...

SQUEEZING THE RUBBER TIGHTLY ON THE LINE, I PULL IT THROUGH TWO OR THREE TIMES AS NECESSARY AND REMOVE ALL THE KINKS. YOUR TURN NOW!

Extracting a hook

A tip guard for hooks

Storing nylon line

WHAT'S IN THIS BAG, GEORGE?

NEW SPOOLS OF NYLON LINE. IF NYLON LINE IS LEFT EXPOSED TOO LONG TO THE LIGHT IT WILL DETERIORATE. SO I KEEP IT IN A BLACK BAG TO PRESERVE ITS STRENGTH.

LOOK HOW STRONG THIS IS — AND I'VE HAD IT FOR MONTHS.

I PUT THE SPOOLS IN AND CLOSE IT TIGHTLY. I DO THE SAME AT HOME TO KEEP MY LINE IN PERFECT CONDITION.

Marking a fly reel

WHAT'S HAPPENED TO YOUR FLY CASTING TODAY, JOHN... WHAT WEIGHT IS YOUR LINE?

IT MUST BE A No.6... NO, PERHAPS A No.5. I'M NOT REALLY SURE.

I'D SAY IT'S A No.5 BUT WHY DON'T YOU MARK THE LINE WEIGHT ON THE REEL

DT 4 F
DT 5 F
WF 3 F
WF 7 S

WRITE IT ON A PIECE OF TAPE AND STICK IT ON THE REEL DRUM. LOOK AT THE WAY I'VE DONE IT.

Loops on wire traces—making the loop

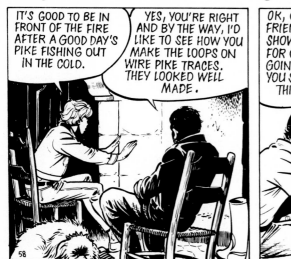

Threading a sleeve on to a wire trace

Sharpening hooks

Keeping tied hooks tidy

Terminal tackle

Your tackle box may be full of all the right equipment and, in theory, you may know just how to use it. But there's no substitute for experience in fishing—except perhaps profiting from the experience of others. This chapter will help you decide among other things when to use a paternoster leger rig, which bite indicator to use in windy weather or how to keep a livebait alive and working.

Shock absorber for leger weight

OH NO! I'VE BROKEN MY LINE BUT I WASN'T PULLING ALL THAT HARD ON THE FISH!

JUDGING BY WHERE THE BREAK OCCURRED, I THINK YOUR LINE MUST HAVE WORN WHERE YOU'VE BEEN STRIKING AGAINST THE LEGER WEIGHT.

65

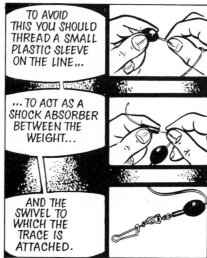

TO AVOID THIS YOU SHOULD THREAD A SMALL PLASTIC SLEEVE ON THE LINE...

...TO ACT AS A SHOCK ABSORBER BETWEEN THE WEIGHT...

AND THE SWIVEL TO WHICH THE TRACE IS ATTACHED.

YOU SEE! THAT ONE DIDN'T BREAK ON ME.

WE HAVEN'T FINISHED YET!

Stop knot for sliding float

THIS STOP KNOT'S A NUISANCE...IT DOESN'T ALWAYS STAY IN THE RIGHT PLACE AND ONCE OR TWICE THE FLOAT HAS SLIPPED OVER IT.

COME HERE, JOHN, AND I'LL SHOW YOU WHAT TO DO.

66

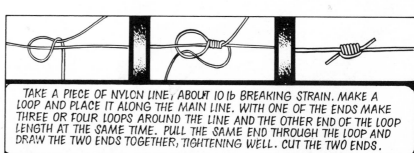

TAKE A PIECE OF NYLON LINE, ABOUT 10 lb BREAKING STRAIN. MAKE A LOOP AND PLACE IT ALONG THE MAIN LINE. WITH ONE OF THE ENDS MAKE THREE OR FOUR LOOPS AROUND THE LINE AND THE OTHER END OF THE LOOP LENGTH AT THE SAME TIME. PULL THE SAME END THROUGH THE LOOP AND DRAW THE TWO ENDS TOGETHER, TIGHTENING WELL. CUT THE TWO ENDS.

HEY, GEORGE, THIS KNOT'S TERRIFIC! I MADE A GOOD CAST AND MY FLOAT IS IN THE RIGHT POSITION ON THE LINE NOW.

Bite indicators

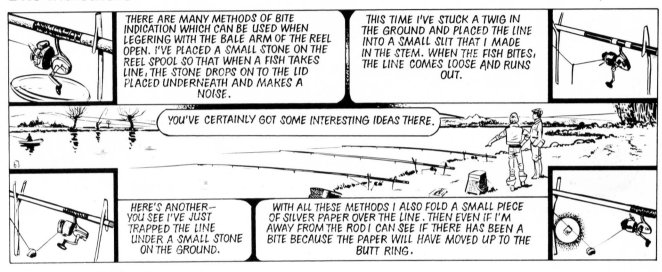

THERE ARE MANY METHODS OF BITE INDICATION WHICH CAN BE USED WHEN LEGERING WITH THE BALE ARM OF THE REEL OPEN. I'VE PLACED A SMALL STONE ON THE REEL SPOOL SO THAT WHEN A FISH TAKES LINE, THE STONE DROPS ON TO THE LID PLACED UNDERNEATH AND MAKES A NOISE.

THIS TIME I'VE STUCK A TWIG IN THE GROUND AND PLACED THE LINE INTO A SMALL SLIT THAT I MADE IN THE STEM. WHEN THE FISH BITES, THE LINE COMES LOOSE AND RUNS OUT.

YOU'VE CERTAINLY GOT SOME INTERESTING IDEAS THERE.

HERE'S ANOTHER— YOU SEE I'VE JUST TRAPPED THE LINE UNDER A SMALL STONE ON THE GROUND.

WITH ALL THESE METHODS I ALSO FOLD A SMALL PIECE OF SILVER PAPER OVER THE LINE. THEN EVEN IF I'M AWAY FROM THE ROD I CAN SEE IF THERE HAS BEEN A BITE BECAUSE THE PAPER WILL HAVE MOVED UP TO THE BUTT RING.

Bite indicators for windy weather

THERE'S NEARLY A GALE BLOWING TODAY, GEORGE—I DON'T THINK ANY OF YOUR BITE INDICATORS WOULD BE MUCH GOOD IN THIS WEATHER.

YOU'RE TOO RIGHT, JOHN AND I KNOW JUST THE THING FOR THESE CONDITIONS.

YOU SIMPLY PLACE AN ELASTIC BAND OVER THE ROD HANDLE JUST IN FRONT OF THE REEL FITTING. THEN HAVING CAST OUT YOUR LEGER RIG, YOU TIGHTEN UP TO THE WEIGHT, OPEN THE BALE ARM OF THE REEL AND TUCK A SMALL LOOP OF LINE UNDER THE ELASTIC BAND.

THIS STOPS THE WIND PULLING LINE OF THE REEL AND WHEN A FISH BITES IT TUGS THE LOOP FREE.

WHAT A JOLLY GOOD IDEA, GEORGE!

Paternoster leger rig

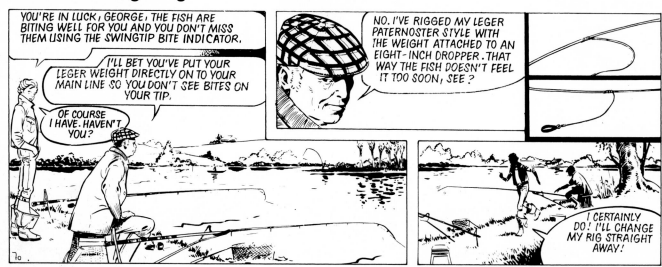

Fast river legering

Preparing weights

I'VE BOUGHT A NEW SUPPLY OF OLIVETTE TYPE WEIGHTS, GEORGE. I'M PREPARED FOR ANYTHING

I SEE. NOW WE MUST GET THEM READY.

GET THEM READY? FOR WHAT?

FIRST, THERE MIGHT BE ROUGH SURFACES NEEDING ATTENTION IN THE HOLE THROUGH THE CENTRE, AND THEN YOU MUST OPEN UP THE ENDS SLIGHTLY SO THAT THE LINE WILL SLIDE THROUGH EASILY. WITH A BIG NEEDLE, IT ONLY TAKES A MINUTE.

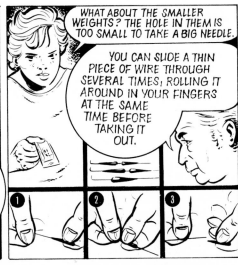

WHAT ABOUT THE SMALLER WEIGHTS? THE HOLE IN THEM IS TOO SMALL TO TAKE A BIG NEEDLE.

YOU CAN SLIDE A THIN PIECE OF WIRE THROUGH SEVERAL TIMES, ROLLING IT AROUND IN YOUR FINGERS AT THE SAME TIME BEFORE TAKING IT OUT.

① ② ③

Livebaiting

MY LIVEBAIT IS DEAD ALREADY. IT SEEMS TO HAVE BEEN DAMAGED BY THE BARB ON THE HOOK.

MINE IS STILL LIVELY— LOOK HOW WELL IT'S WORKING. COME AND SEE WHY— I'VE GOT TO CHECK IT ANYWAY.

YOU SEE! I PROTECTED ITS MOUTH WITH A TINY PIECE OF RUBBER FROM AN OLD INNER TUBE

BAIT YOUR HOOK NORMALLY, THEN FORCE THE PIECE OF RUBBER OVER THE POINT AND BELOW THE BARB, LIKE THIS.

Tying a dropper knot

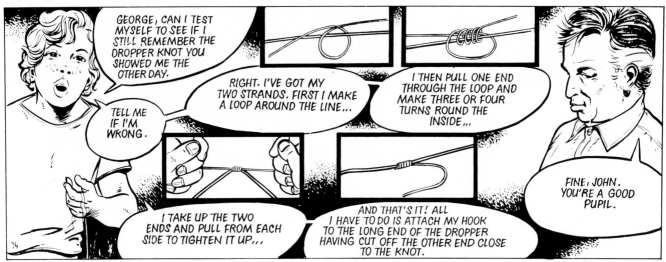

Tackle and fly boxes

Repairs and odd jobs

Inside every angler there should be a handyman able to cope with the many small expected, or unexpected, jobs which can be necessary either when preparing for your fishing trip, on the river bank or back home again with your catch.

Restoring a worn fly

WHAT ARE YOU DOING, GEORGE?

I'M RESTORING THE ATTRACTIVENESS OF THIS WELL-USED FLY.

IT WAS QUITE OUT OF SHAPE, RATHER DIRTY AND GREASY. BUT THE STEAM CLEANS IT UP.

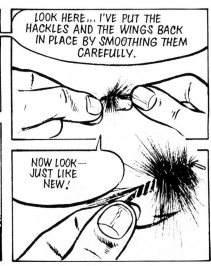

LOOK HERE... I'VE PUT THE HACKLES AND THE WINGS BACK IN PLACE BY SMOOTHING THEM CAREFULLY.

NOW LOOK — JUST LIKE NEW!

Tidy swivels

ALL THESE CLIP SWIVELS GET MIXED UP IN MY TACKLE BOX. I PICK UP ONE AND THEY ALL COME OUT, AND THEN SOME GET LOST IN THE GRASS.

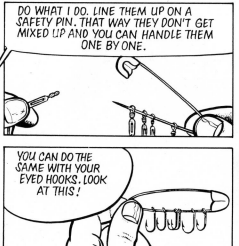

DO WHAT I DO. LINE THEM UP ON A SAFETY PIN. THAT WAY THEY DON'T GET MIXED UP AND YOU CAN HANDLE THEM ONE BY ONE.

YOU CAN DO THE SAME WITH YOUR EYED HOOKS. LOOK AT THIS!

Making a float—cutting out

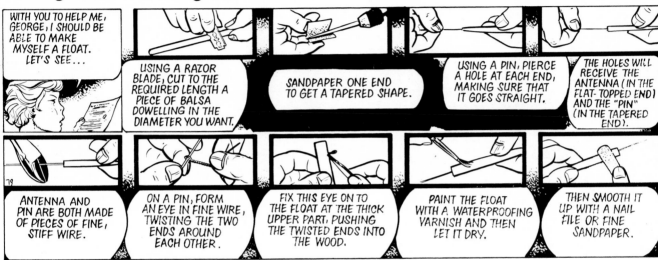

WITH YOU TO HELP ME, GEORGE, I SHOULD BE ABLE TO MAKE MYSELF A FLOAT. LET'S SEE...

USING A RAZOR BLADE, CUT TO THE REQUIRED LENGTH A PIECE OF BALSA DOWELLING IN THE DIAMETER YOU WANT.

SANDPAPER ONE END TO GET A TAPERED SHAPE.

USING A PIN, PIERCE A HOLE AT EACH END, MAKING SURE THAT IT GOES STRAIGHT.

THE HOLES WILL RECEIVE THE ANTENNA (IN THE FLAT-TOPPED END) AND THE "PIN" (IN THE TAPERED END).

ANTENNA AND PIN ARE BOTH MADE OF PIECES OF FINE, STIFF WIRE.

ON A PIN, FORM AN EYE IN FINE WIRE, TWISTING THE TWO ENDS AROUND EACH OTHER.

FIX THIS EYE ON TO THE FLOAT AT THE THICK UPPER PART, PUSHING THE TWISTED ENDS INTO THE WOOD.

PAINT THE FLOAT WITH A WATERPROOFING VARNISH AND THEN LET IT DRY.

THEN SMOOTH IT UP WITH A NAIL FILE OR FINE SANDPAPER.

Making a float—finishing off

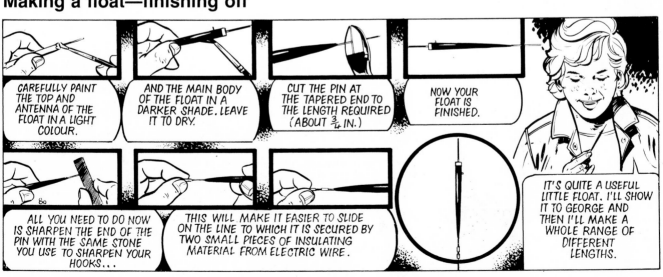

CAREFULLY PAINT THE TOP AND ANTENNA OF THE FLOAT IN A LIGHT COLOUR.

AND THE MAIN BODY OF THE FLOAT IN A DARKER SHADE. LEAVE IT TO DRY.

CUT THE PIN AT THE TAPERED END TO THE LENGTH REQUIRED (ABOUT $\frac{3}{4}$ IN.)

NOW YOUR FLOAT IS FINISHED.

IT'S QUITE A USEFUL LITTLE FLOAT. I'LL SHOW IT TO GEORGE AND THEN I'LL MAKE A WHOLE RANGE OF DIFFERENT LENGTHS.

ALL YOU NEED TO DO NOW IS SHARPEN THE END OF THE PIN WITH THE SAME STONE YOU USE TO SHARPEN YOUR HOOKS...

THIS WILL MAKE IT EASIER TO SLIDE ON THE LINE TO WHICH IT IS SECURED BY TWO SMALL PIECES OF INSULATING MATERIAL FROM ELECTRIC WIRE.

A cheap bailer

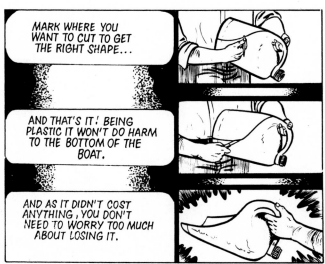

Interchangeable float caps

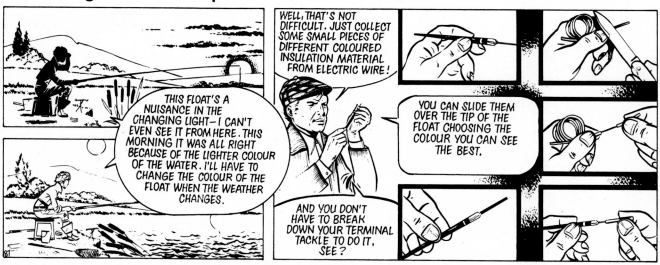

A minnow trap

IS THIS THE PLASTIC BOTTLE YOU'RE USING TO MAKE YOUR MINNOW TRAP?

THAT'S IT, JOHN. IT DOES THE JOB VERY WELL

FIRST I CUT IT THROUGH, JUST BELOW THE NECK.

THEN I TURN THE NECK UPSIDE DOWN AND FORCE IT INTO THE BOTTLE.

I MAKE A FEW HOLES IN THE BOTTOM TO ALLOW THE WATER TO FLOW THROUGH AND THAT'S IT!

BUT YOU HAVE TO REMEMBER TO WEIGHT IT DOWN WITH A STONE AT THE BOTTOM OF THE RIVER, DON'T YOU, SO IT DOESN'T FLOAT AWAY? ONE GOOD THING, THOUGH, IS THAT IT WON'T BREAK LIKE GLASS WOULD.

Keep hooks rust free

I'M FED UP WITH FINDING MY HOOKS RUSTING UP IN BOXES AND TINS. HOW CAN I STORE THEM, GEORGE?

TRY THESE CARDBOARD STRIPS. JUST LAY THE HOOKS IN ROWS ON THE CARDBOARD AND PLACE A STRIP OF SELLOTAPE OVER THEM.

WHEN YOU WANT TO USE ONE OF THEM, YOU PEEL BACK THE TAPE SUFFICIENTLY TO LIFT OFF THE HOOK. EASY ISN'T IT?

Forceps at the ready

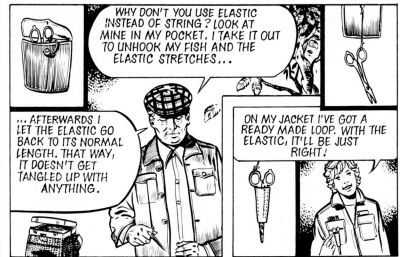

When maggots turn

Leaky waders

Leaky boots

Repairing rubber boots

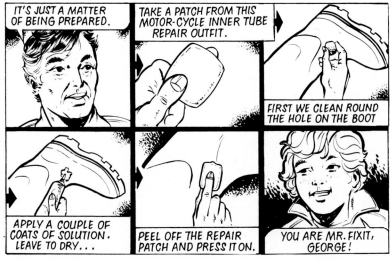

A do-it-yourself plummet

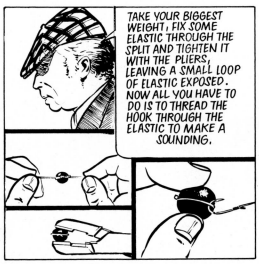

A handy bait box

GEORGE, LOOK! I'VE BROUGHT THE PLASTIC CONTAINER YOU WANTED. YOU TOLD ME YOU'D MAKE A BAIT BOX WITH IT.

WE'LL DO IT STRAIGHT AWAY, JOHN.

FIRST OF ALL I MARK THE CUTTING LEVEL WITH A FELT PEN ACCORDING TO THE DEPTH REQUIRED.
NOW I CUT CAREFULLY, FOLLOWING THE LINE WITH A KNIFE.
ALL I NEED TO DO NOW IS EVEN UP THE EDGES AND MY GROUNDBAIT BOX IS READY! IT'S LIGHT TO CARRY AROUND AND EASILY WASHABLE. IT MAKES AN IDEAL BAIT BOX THAT COSTS NEXT TO NOTHING!

Don't lose your sunglasses

I'VE JUST FOUND MY SUNGLASSES IN THE GRASS. THEY MUST HAVE FALLEN OFF WHEN I SLIPPED, SO I WAS LUCKY TO GET THEM BACK AGAIN.

I SEE THAT YOU'VE STILL GOT THEM PUSHED UP ON TOP OF YOUR HEAD, JUST AS BEFORE...

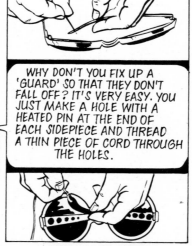

WHY DON'T YOU FIX UP A 'GUARD' SO THAT THEY DON'T FALL OFF? IT'S VERY EASY. YOU JUST MAKE A HOLE WITH A HEATED PIN AT THE END OF EACH SIDEPIECE AND THREAD A THIN PIECE OF CORD THROUGH THE HOLES.

THAT WAY, WHEN YOU DON'T NEED TO WEAR THEM, THEY STILL HANG AROUND YOUR NECK.

Mounting a pike head—preparation

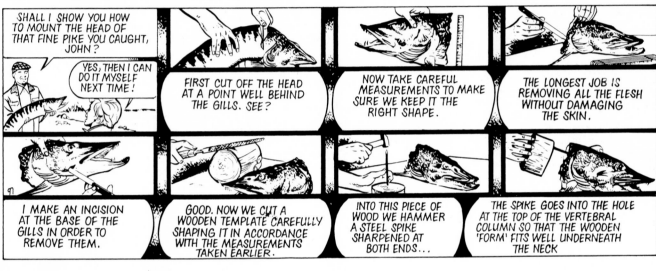

Mounting a pike head—the mount

Reading the water

Fishing always has an element of luck, but you can improve your success rate by studying the habits of the fish. You can recognise the spots where the fish are most likely to be, in a river or a lake. Observe the depth of the water, the speed of the current and the bankside vegetation and weedbeds to see whether there are carp, barbel or chub lurking there.

Spotting likely hotspots

I CAN HARDLY WAIT TO GET BACK ON THE BANK—IT SEEMS AGES SINCE I HELD A ROD.

WELL, JOHN—ONLY ANOTHER WEEK OF THE CLOSE SEASON TO GO AND THEN WE CAN START FISHING AGAIN.

TELL YOU WHAT WE **CAN** DO—WE'LL WALK AROUND OUR LOCAL WATERS AND PICK OUT SOME LIKELY 'HOTSPOTS' TO TRY NEXT WEEK.

NOW, JOHN, I'M GOING TO SHOW YOU WHERE TO LOOK FOR PARTICULAR KINDS OF FISH— THEY ALL HAVE THEIR FAVOURITE PLACES.

Where to find perch

NOW HERE WE SHOULD FIND A FEW PERCH—THOSE SPINY FISH WITH THE HANDSOME STRIPES.

WHY DO THEY STAY AROUND THESE PLACES?

WELL, PERCH FEED MAINLY ON SMALLER FISH AND HERE THEY CAN LIE IN WAIT FOR THEM HIDDEN AWAY IN THE DARK CORNERS AND CREVICES IN THE STONEWORK.

SOMETIMES YOU CAN SPOT WHEN BIG PERCH ARE AROUND BECAUSE YOU SEE LITTLE FISH JUMPING OUT OF THE WATER TO ESCAPE THEM.

Where to find carp and tench

Where to find dace

Where to find chub

Where to find roach

Glossary

ARLESEY BOMB
Pear-shaped leger weight fitted with a swivel.

BALE ARM
Fitted to a fixed spool reel, it revolves and lays line on the spool as the handle is turned.

BULLET
Round leger weight with a hole drilled through the centre.

BUTT
The handle end of the fishing rod.

CASTER
The chrysalid of the maggot; used as a hookbait.

CENTRE PIN
Type of reel

DISGORGER
Fork-ended instrument used to remove the hook from a fish's throat.

DOUGH BOBBIN
Small ball of breadpaste squeezed on to the line near the butt as a bite indicator.

FRY
Young fish

GROUNDBAIT
Moistened mixture of breadcrumbs, bran or other cereals introduced into the water to attract fish.

HEMPSEED
Small black seeds which are stewed before use as hookbait or groundbait.

HOOK LENGTH
The short piece of nylon line to which a hook is tied.

KEEP NET
Long, ringed net into which fish are placed when caught.

LANDING NET
Net on a triangular or circular frame attached to a long handle, used for lifting a hooked fish from the water.

LEGER
Style of fishing in which a weight, running on the line, anchors the terminal gear on the bottom.

LOBWORMS
Ordinary garden worms used as bait.

PATERNOSTER
Terminal tackle with the hook length attached to the main line above the weight.

ROD REST
Stick with a forked end, stuck into bank, on which the rod may be placed.

SNAP TACKLE
Treble hooks attached to wire used to present a live or deadbait for pike fishing.

SPLIT SHOT
Small balls of lead split on one side to enable them to be squeezed on to the line under a float.

STRIKE
Sharp upwards or sideways movement of the rod made when a bite is observed.

SWIM
The area of water within reach of the angler's tackle from his chosen spot on the bank.

SWIMFEEDER
Plastic or metal container from which groundbait can be introduced adjacent to the angler's hookbait.

SWINGTIP
Flexible attachment to the rod tip which gives delicate bite indication when legering.

TARES
Small, dried peas which are soaked and used as hookbait.

TRAIL
The length of line (or trace) between leger weight and hook.

TROTTING
Allowing float tackle to travel down the river at the speed of the current.

Metrication

Metrication
Metric weights and measures are becoming more widely used for fishing tackle, so a few guidelines for quick, approximate conversion can help.

Rod lengths
1 metre is just over 39 inches and 2½ centimetres is 1 inch, so an 11 ft rod measures approximately 3.38 metres and a 10 ft rod 3.07 metres.

Weights
28 grams equal approximately 1 ounce and 1,000 grams (or 1 kilogram) just under 2¼ pounds. So a half ounce leger weight would be about 14 grams and a three quarter ounce lead about 21 grams. And if you want to measure your catch metrically, a one pound roach would be about 450 grams.

Line strength
Breaking strains for nylon fishing line are usually marked in pounds and the line diameter in millimetres. Here is a short table for converting pounds into millimetres. (Slight variations occur with different makes of line.)

lbs (breaking strain)	mm (line diameter)
1.5	0.10
2.0	0.12
2.9	0.15
4.8	0.20
7.9	0.25
9.7	0.30
13.0	0.35

Photographs

Page 8. A properly maintained reel will give accurate, long-distance casting.

13. The bale arm is a delicate mechanism, so handle it with care.

17. The angler selects a likely spot and casts.

18. Playing the waiting game.

23. Testing time for tackle.

27. Netting a still-water bream.

29. Baitfishing for trout in a mountain stream.

30. Coloured maggots are considered to be very attractive to fish.

35. Loading a catapult for long distance groundbaiting.

39. A picturesque roach swim on the River Kennet.

43. Not too wet, not too dry. Squeezing a ball of groundbait to get it just right.

46. Everything in its place—Ray Mumford's tackle box.

51. Former world champion, Ian Heaps with his world record match catch of 166 lbs.

55. Hooking up a deadbait.

57. Sorting out hooks and lines for the next fishing trip.

58. A match angler with his equipment positioned within easy reach.

63. Ray Thwaites with a magnificent 30 lb pike.

66. An early season tench is returned to the water.

71. Sheltering behind their umbrellas, a row of match anglers on a Sussex drain.

73. Whipping on a rod ring.

75. A beaten pike comes to the net.

77. Preparing groundbait from breadcrusts.

79. Admiring glances for an 18 lb pike.

82. A good fish safely in the landing net.

85. Watertight waders are a must for this sort of fishing.

87. Sweetcorn bait to tempt carp.

89. A well-mounted pike's head makes a splendid souvenir.

All colour photographs by W. Howes

Biography

A well-known angling journalist, Fred Rashbrook was for ten years Managing Editor of *Angler's Mail*, a national weekly newspaper widely read by followers of all branches of the sport.
He has also been involved in the production of a number of angling books and has a wide practical experience of fishing in the British Isles and abroad.